# Dog

Written by
**Matthew Rayner** BVetMed MRCVS

Photographed by
**Jane Burton**

**Gareth Stevens Publishing**
A WORLD ALMANAC EDUCATION GROUP COMPANY

Please visit our web site at: www.garethstevens.com
For a free color catalog describing Gareth Stevens
Publishing's list of high-quality books and multi-
media programs, call 1-800-542-2595 (USA)
or 1-800-387-3178 (Canada). Gareth Stevens
Publishing's fax: (414) 332-3567.

**Picture credits**
t=top, b=bottom, m=middle, l=left, r=right
All photographs by Jane Burton except for the following:
Warren Photographic: 5r, 6b, 6–7b, 7t, 8–9b, 9t, 11tl,
11tr, 12t, 13t, 4mb, 18lt, 18lb, 20m, 23br, 26m, 26–27b,
28b, 29tr, 29m, 29mr.

**Library of Congress Cataloging-in-Publication Data**

Rayner, Matthew.
    Dog / written by Matthew Rayner; photographed
by Jane Burton. — North American ed.
      p. cm. — (I am your pet)
    Includes bibliographical references and index.
    Summary: Presents simple information about
dogs and choosing one as a pet.
    ISBN 0-8368-4103-4 (lib. bdg.)
    1. Dogs—Juvenile literature. [1. Dogs.
2. Pets.] I. Burton, Jane, ill. II. Title.
SF426.5.R38    2004
636.7—dc22        2003066152

This North American edition first published in 2004 by
**Gareth Stevens Publishing**
A World Almanac Education Group Company
330 West Olive Street, Suite 100
Milwaukee, WI 53212 USA

Original edition copyright © 2004 Bookwork Ltd.,
Unit 17, Piccadilly Mill, Lower Street, Stroud,
Gloucestershire, GL5 2HT, United Kingdom.

Editorial Director: Louise Pritchard
Editor: Annabel Blackledge
Design Director: Jill Plank
Art Editor: Kate Mullins
Gareth Stevens Editor: Jenette Donovan Guntly
Gareth Stevens Designer: Kami M. Koenig

Printed in the United States of America

1 2 3 4 5 6 7 8 9 08 07 06 05 04

Now then, where should I start?

# Contents

4    Doggy data

6    Different dogs

8    Running wild

10    Are you ready?

12    Pick a pooch

14    Dog's dinner

16    Talk to me

18    Good dog!

20    Playtime!

22    Let's walk

24    Healthy hound

26    A dog's best friend

28    Puppy love

30    Glossary

31    Find out more . . .

32    Index

Words that appear in the glossary are printed in **boldface** type the first time they are used in the text.

# Doggy data

**Search dogs**
Some of my friends use their sense of smell to find people that need rescuing. They find bombs and drugs, too. They think it is a game.

**Great mover**
I have powerful muscles that allow me to move my body in all directions.

**Furry coat**
My coat has two layers. The fur near my skin is shorter and softer than the fur on top.

**Family ties**
I belong to a large family of animals called **canines**. The first canines were wolves, and I behave like a wolf in many ways. Foxes and jackals are just two of my other canine cousins.

**Tail talk**
I use my tail to show my feelings and talk to other dogs. It also helps me to balance when I am running fast.

**Mmmm, you smell good to me!**

**Meat eater**
My teeth are
sharp and pointed
for eating meat
and chewing bones.

## Super senses

Like you, I have five senses. These are
smell, hearing, sight, touch, and taste.
Smell is important to me. I learn about
the dogs I meet by smelling them. My
sense of smell is better than yours.
My hearing is better than yours, too.
I often hear noises that you do not hear.

**Paws and claws**
I have tough pads on the underside of
my paws. They protect my feet when I
run on rough ground. The claws on the
end of my toes help me grip the ground.

**My mom and dad**
My parents were
not the same
kind, or **breed**,
of dog. Most dog
breeds look very
different from
each other.

**What a mix-up!**
I am a mixture of Border collie
and shih tzu breeds. I am known
as a **mongrel** or crossbreed.

**A mongrel and proud of it!**
Mongrels like me are often much healthier
than **purebred** dogs and we usually live longer.
We are also just as friendly and playful!

# Different dogs

## All sorts
There are more than 100 breeds
of pet dog. Some of my friends are
heavier than a person. Others are
smaller than a cat. Some
have very long fur
and a few have
no fur at all!

**Small but beautiful**
This is a small breed of dog
called a shih tzu. His early
**ancestors** were from Tibet.
It is cold there, which is
why he has long, thick fur.

# From little things ...

Some puppies grow up to be large (24 inches or 61 centimeters tall at the shoulder) or medium-size dogs (18 to 24 inches or 46 to 61 cm tall). Some dogs stay small (less than 18 inches or 46 cm tall).

**Larger than life**
These puppies are Labradors. They will be large dogs.

I think I am just the right size.

**Happy medium**
This friend of mine is a basset hound puppy. She will grow up to be a medium-size dog.

## Wild living

Wolves live in groups called packs. The packs are led by a head male and female wolf. Wolves protect their packs from other wolves and animals.

### My pack

I treat you as part of my pack. When we go for a walk, I think we are hunting for food. If I bark at a visitor, I am only guarding my pack.

# Running wild

### Pack of pets

When pet dogs live together, one is the leader of the pack. The others always do what the leader says.

### LOOK OUT!

- **Some dogs** fight with other dogs they meet because they think they need to protect their pack.
- **Even pet** dogs might decide to go hunting, as wolves do. Always put me on a leash near farm animals, especially sheep.

### Who is boss?

Dogs like to play together. Even in a game, there is a boss. This stops real fights from starting.

# Wild relations

Foxes are found all over the world.
You may have seen fox cubs play fighting,
just like I play with my friends. It is good
hunting practice for foxes, but for pets
like me, it is just good fun.

**Only fun**
When we play fight,
we can make a lot of
noise, but we do not
hurt each other.

Okay, okay . . .
I give up!

## First things first

Before you bring me home, you will need to buy me a bed, collar, leash, proper dog food, brushes, and toys. I will also need an identity tag with my telephone number and address and the telephone number of my **veterinarian**, or vet, as well.

# Are you ready?

## Brushing up

There are many kinds of dog brushes and combs. I have long fur so you should **groom** me with a comb or metal brush. Rubber brushes or brushes with short bristles are good for dogs with short fur.

Now what am I supposed to do?

## House training

You must teach a puppy where she is allowed to go to the bathroom. This is called house training. She will use a lot of newspapers before she learns to go to the bathroom outside!

## My own bed

It is important that I have my own bed. I will be in it most of the day! I would like a large basket or box with a blanket or rug. A bean bag is comfortable, too, but make sure I do not chew it.

### Cry baby

I might cry a bit during the night at first. This is normal. It is best to ignore me. Otherwise, I will learn that I just have to cry to make you come to see me.

# Pick a

**Different characters**
We all have different characters. Some puppies are lively and some are quiet and shy.

## Where to go

If you want a purebred puppy, go to a breeder. If you would like a puppy or an older dog and do not mind what breed you have, get one of my friends from an animal shelter. You will be helping a lonely dog.

**Choices, choices**
Take your time choosing a puppy. There are more than 150 breeds of dogs to choose from!

### LOOK OUT!
• **Avoid buying** a puppy or dog from a pet shop or **puppy mill**. He may have been treated badly and could be sick.
• **Make sure** you take a puppy to the vet for a full checkup.

## Home sweet home

Different breeds of dogs are suitable for different homes. Ask your vet which breed would be best for your home and lifestyle.

# Pooch

## Peak condition

Before you take home a dog or puppy, make sure he looks healthy. He should have clear eyes and a clean, healthy coat.

**Looks aren't everything**
A dog's personality is very important. Be sure you choose a dog that is playful, happy, and active.

**Older and wiser**
Most grown-up dogs will settle quickly into a new home.

### Room for growth

Small dogs are fully grown at about one year old. Large dogs are not fully grown until nearly two years old. By then, they may be bigger than you!

How could you resist me?

# What I need to eat

I like to eat meat best, but I am not fussy and will probably eat anything you give me. The best food for you to feed me is ready-made dog food. It contains everything I need. It comes in cans or as dry nuggets.

# Dog's dinner

### Eating habits

Please give me one or two meals a day, in a nice clean bowl. I like to eat by myself. I do not want even my friends to take my food.

Dry food

Dog biscuits

Canned wet food

Chewy treats

Treated bone

### Safe snacks

I love nibbling on bones, but they can be dangerous. They can splinter in my tummy and make me sick. Treated bones from pet shops are the safest kind.

# Hungry hound

Different-size dogs need different amounts of food. Check the can or bag to find out how much I need. If I am really good, you could give me a dog biscuit or a chewy treat.

**Thirsty work**
If I play a lot or eat dry food, I will drink lots of water every day.

All that playing has made me thirsty!

# Drink up!
I must always be able to find clean water to drink. If possible, let me have bowls of water inside and outside my home. Keep an eye on my water bowls. Make sure they are clean and full of water.

## Doggy language

Dogs talk to each other using different parts of their bodies. I will talk to you this way, too. As you spend time with me, you will learn my **body language** and will understand what I am saying.

# Talk to me

### Don't beg
I know I should not beg for food, but I will try anyway. I will sit or stand by you when you are eating and wag my tail. I will probably dribble. Tell me to go away.

### Feeling frightened
If I am really scared, I will push my ears back against my head and hold my tail between my legs. Be careful, because I may bite to protect myself.

### Play with me
I hope you will play games with me. When I want to play, I will bring you toys and wag my tail. If I "play bow," with my front legs down on the ground and my bottom in the air, I am in a really playful mood!

**Tickle on the tummy**
I will roll over if I want you to scratch my tummy.

# I will not fight
When I am playing with other dogs, I may roll over on my back. I am telling them that I will not hurt them. I just want to play. This stops a game from turning into a fight.

## LOOK OUT!
- **If I curl** up my lips and show my teeth, it means I may bite.
- **I may jump** up at visitors to make them talk to me. This is not good. The visitors should ignore me.
- **Be careful** when I am eating. If I think you are going to take away my food, I may growl to tell you I am mad.

## Lots to learn

I am smart, but I need to be trained to do things right. I am easy to train, especially if I think it is a game. You can take me to training classes. Puppy classes are good when I am young. They will help me to get used to other dogs and people.

**LOOK OUT!**
- **Do not** let me off the leash on a walk until you are sure I will come back when you call me. Never let me off the leash near a road.

Can I have my treat now?

# Good dog!

### Clicker training
A good way to train me is with a **clicker**. I will learn to sit or lie down when you click it.

### Just rewards
I am easy to train if I get a reward when I do something right. Give me a small treat and tell me how good I am.

**Paying attention**
I love learning tricks. Make sure you have my full attention before teaching me something new.

# The basic lessons

Even if you do not want to teach me lots of tricks, you must teach me some basic **commands**. Teach me to sit, lie down, stay, and come when I am called. I should always come to you when you call me.

**Bad dog!**
Never yell or hit me if I have done something wrong. I will not understand what you are saying. If I have been bad, just ignore me. Give me lots of praise when I am good again.

**Little by little**
Do not try to teach me too much at once — teach me just a little at a time.

## Games and toys

The more toys I have, the better. They will keep me out of trouble. Most toys from pet shops are great for me to play with, but make sure they are not too small. I could swallow them.

# Playtime!

**Puppy play**
Puppies want to chew everything! If they have plenty of toys, they can chew them instead of things that may harm them.

**Take your pick!**
Different dogs enjoy different games. Some dogs like playing hide-and-seek with toys. Some like a tug-of-war and some like playing fetch.

Do you want to play tug-of-war with me?

**Rope toys**
Rope toys are good for playing tug-of-war. They are safe for me and they also help keep my teeth clean.

**I can smell food**
You can get a special ball and put food in it for me. See how long it takes me to get out all the food.

# Keep me amused

Do not leave me by myself for too long. If I get bored, I may chew things that I should not. Give me lots of toys to play with. Put on the television or radio if you go out. The voices will keep me company.

## Daily exercise

I need exercise every day. It keeps me healthy and stops me from getting fat. Let me get used to being on a leash at home before you take me out. I must never go out without wearing my collar and identity tag.

### Runaway!

If I do not come when you call, do not run after me. I will think it is a game. Offer me some food. When I do come back, put on my leash and take me straight home.

### Long leash

A leash that you can make longer and shorter is a good one to use on my walks. Then, you never have to let me off of my leash. Be careful near roads, in case I run in front of a car.

# Let's Walk

## Scoop it up

If you walk me along the pavement or in a public park, you must clean up any mess I make. Dog mess can cause nasty diseases. You can use special plastic bags or a dog pooper scooper. I would clean it up myself if I could!

# Safety first

If you take me out when it is dark, make sure I can be seen easily. You can get me a glow-in-the-dark collar or a flashing light to put on my ordinary collar.

**You won't miss me in this!**

### Not too tight
Put on my collar so that it fits loosely, but make sure that I will not be able to pull my head through it.

### Heel!
Teach me to walk by your side. Say, "Heel." If I pull on my leash, I might hurt my neck or pull you over.

### Pull-along dog
If I do pull a lot on the leash, try using a special collar that goes over my nose. If I get too far in front of you, it bends my head down and makes me stop pulling.

# I need you to look after me

I can look after myself quite well, but I need you to keep an eye on me. Take me to the vet for **vaccinations** and **worming** and if you think I am not very well.

# Healthy hound

### Signs of sickness

Take me to the vet if I stop eating or do not want to go for my usual walks. I should also see the vet if I start scratching a lot or drinking more water than I usually do.

**Cleaning my teeth**
Keep my teeth clean by giving me things to chew. You can clean my teeth with my own toothbrush, too.

**Well brushed**
Groom your dog often.
I have long fur so I
must be brushed
every day.

**Feel the feet**
After a walk, check my
paws. Carefully pull
out anything that is
stuck in a pad or
between my toes.

**Bright eyes**
Check my eyes to make sure
they are not runny or red.

# Daily checkup
It is important that you give me
a checkup every day. You may
discover that I am hiding an
illness or injury from you.

**Ear, ear**
Check that my ears are
clean and that they do not
look sore anywhere.

## LOOK OUT!
• **Never put** anything in my ears, even if they
need cleaning or if there is something down
there. Ask my vet for advice and help.
• **Do not throw** sticks for me. They can get
stuck in my throat or cut my mouth.

# Having friends is fun

Wolves live in packs, and pet dogs like company, too. We will live with other dogs and with people. We also can be friends with other animals. It is best if we meet when we are young.

A dog's

Oh, is this your carrot?

**Bunny buddy**
Dogs and rabbits can be friends.

**Keep an eye on us**
You can leave a dog alone with other dogs and cats that they know. Never leave a dog with a rabbit, guinea pig, or a hamster. He may think it is food!

**Your best friend**
You will always be my best friend if you feed me, take me for walks, and play with me. As long as I get lots of exercise, I promise I will not be too naughty.

# best friend

I can't kiss you. I am too sleepy!

## Twice as nice

Two dogs can be twice as much fun as one. But they will be twice as messy! They will keep each other company when you are not at home.

**Double trouble**
Two dogs nearly always get along fine together.

# Puppy love

No help at all
The father does
not help to look
after his puppies.

## Having puppies

Female dogs are good mothers. They will
not need much help from you. They can
have between four and ten puppies, but
the record is twenty-
three. It can take
up to twelve hours
for a female to
give birth to all
of her puppies.

We're
going to have to
find a bigger
home!

**New puppies**
Puppies are
helpless when
they are born.
They are blind
and deaf until
they are about
nine days old.

**Super mom**
The mother
feeds her
puppies with
her milk.

## LOOK OUT!

- **A female** dog can have puppies at six months old. Do not let your dog have puppies unless you are sure you can find good homes for them. The vet can give female and male dogs operations so that they cannot have puppies.

### Father figure
It is interesting to meet the father before buying a puppy, but he may not live in the same home as his puppies.

### Growing up
Puppies grow fast. They will drink milk from their mother for four to five weeks. Then, they can start eating puppy food.

### Puppy chaos!
Puppies just eat, sleep, and play. They will play with each other and with their mother. They will try to eat everything, so keep dangerous things out of their reach.

# Ready to move on
Most puppies are ready for new homes when they are about eight weeks old. To begin with, a puppy will be sad to leave his mother and his brothers and sisters. When he realizes he has a new family and a nice home, he will be fine.

# Glossary

**ancestors**
A dog's ancestors are members of his family from a long time ago, further back than grandparents.

**body language**
Dogs use their bodies to show other dogs and people what they are thinking and feeling. This is called body language.

**breed**
A breed is a type or kind of dog. Dalmatians and Cocker Spaniels are just two breeds of dogs.

**canines**
Dogs belong to an animal family called canines. Foxes and wolves are also part of the canine family.

**clicker**
Clickers are used to train dogs. When you click the button on a clicker, it tells the dog he has done something good.

**commands**
Commands are words that you teach your dog, such as "Sit!" or "Stay!" In time, he will learn to do what you ask him to do.

**groom**
When you groom your dog, you are brushing out dirt and tangles.

**mongrel**
A dog can be a mixture of breeds. He is then called a mongrel.

**puppy mill**
A puppy mill is a place that tries to breed too many dogs. Often, the dogs are sick and underfed.

**purebred**
A purebred dog has a family that includes only dogs of the same breed, such as all Dalmatians.

**vaccinations**
A dog needs vaccinations to stop him from getting serious diseases.

**veterinarian**
A veterinarian, or vet, is a doctor for animals. You should take your dog to see a vet if he is sick or injured and for vaccinations.

**worming**
A dog can get worms inside him. These may make him sick. A vet will help you get rid of the worms.

# Find out more . . .

## Web Sites

**www.americanhumane. org/kids/dogs.htm**
This web site created by the American Humane Society offers information about behavior problems, puppy-proofing your home, and learning to play fetch with your best buddy.

**www.animaland.org**
This fun web site for the American Society for the Prevention of Cruelty to Animals (ASPCA) has a pet care guide, games, cartoons, and more!

**www.kidsanddogs. bravepages.com**
This web site offers advice on caring for a dog. It also has lots of stories, quizzes, and jokes, too.

## Books

*How to Talk to Your Dog.* Jean Craighead George (HarperCollins)

*Pet First Aid for Kids!* Craig Jones (Rescue Critters, LLC)

Hey, this stuff looks great!

# Index

**A**

animal shelters   12

**B**

beds   10, 11
beg   16
bite   16, 17
body language
   16–17
bones   5, 14
breeders   12
breeds   6–7, 12
brushes   10, 11

**C**

canines   4
cats   6, 26
chew   11, 20,
   21, 24
collar   10, 22, 23
company   21,
   26–27

**E**

ears   16, 25
exercise   22–23
eyes   13, 25

**F**

fight   8, 9, 17

food   10, 14–15,
   17, 21, 22, 29
foxes   4, 9
fur   4, 6, 11, 25

**G**

grooming   11, 25

**H**

health   12, 13, 22,
   24–25
hearing   5
house training   11
hunting   8

**I**

identity tags
   10, 22

**J**

jackals   4

**L**

leash   10, 22, 23

**P**

packs   8, 26
paws   5, 25
pet shop   12,
   14, 20
play   9, 15, 16, 17,
   20–21

puppy   7, 11, 18,
   20, 26–27
puppy mill   12

**S**

senses   5

**T**

tail   4, 16
teeth   5, 21, 24
toys   10, 16, 20–21
training   18–19
treats   14, 18

**V**

vaccinations   24
veterinarian
   (vet) 10, 12, 24,
   25, 29

**W**

walk   8, 18, 22–23,
   25, 26
water   15
wolves   4, 8, 26